D1613616

SOCCER

by Jonatha A. Brown
Reading consultant: Susan Nations, M.Ed., author/literacy coach/consultant

WEEKLY WR READER®
EARLY LEARNING LIBRARY

Please visit our web site at: **www.earlyliteracy.cc**
For a free color catalog describing Weekly Reader® Early Learning Library's list of high-quality books, call 1-877-445-5824 (USA) or 1-800-387-3178 (Canada). Weekly Reader® Early Learning Library's fax: (414) 336-0164.

Library of Congress Cataloging-in-Publication Data

Brown, Jonatha A.
    Soccer / Jonatha A. Brown.
        p. cm. — (My favorite sport)
    Includes bibliographical references and index.
    ISBN 0-8368-4341-X (lib. bdg.)
    ISBN 0-8368-4348-7 (softcover)
    1. Soccer—Juvenile literature. I. Title.
  GV943.25.B75   2004
  796.334—dc22   2004041993

This edition first published in 2005 by
Weekly Reader® Early Learning Library
330 West Olive Street, Suite 100
Milwaukee, WI 53212 USA   604 90 호

Copyright © 2005 by Weekly Reader® Early Learning Library

Editor: JoAnn Early Macken
Art direction, cover and layout design: Tammy West
Photo research: Diane Laska-Swanke

Photo credits: Cover, title, p. 13, Gregg Andersen; p. 5 © Hulton Archive/Getty Images; p. 6 © Tsafrir Abayov/WireImage.com; p. 7 © AFP/Getty Images; p. 9 Tammy West/© Weekly Reader Early Learning Library, 2005; p. 10 © John Mottern/AFP/Getty Images; p. 11 © Jim Rogash/ WireImage.com; p. 12 © Jamie McDonald/Getty Images; p. 14 © Gary M. Prior/Getty Images; p. 16 © Robert Cianflone/Getty Images; p. 17 © Action Images/WireImage.com; p. 18 © Jaime Schwaberow/R. Clarkson & Assoc./WireImage.com; p. 19 © JoAnn Early Macken; p. 21 © Vincent Laforet/Getty Images

Printed in the United States of America

1 2 3 4 5 6 7 8 9 08 07 06 05 04

Table of Contents

CHAPTER 1

Soccer Then and Now

Soccer is a very old game. In ancient times, it was played in Greece, Rome, and China. Much later, it caught on in Europe. Then it came to North America. Now soccer is the most popular team sport on Earth.

In some places, soccer is called "football." But it is not the same as North American football.

Many people think soccer is the most exciting team sport of all. It is fun for kids to play. It is fun for adults, too. The best amateur players can go on to play as professionals. They get paid to play the game they love.

Players in the 1700s used their hands and feet to play football.

Israeli soccer fans cheer for Brazil in a World Cup game.

Soccer is a great spectator sport, too. Fans of all ages go to games to cheer for their favorite teams. Some soccer fans are very loyal to their favorite teams.

Some of the greatest players become rich and famous. They inspire many young players. Names like Pele and Mia Hamm are known far and wide. They have helped make soccer the popular sport it is today.

Pele dribbles past a defender.

CHAPTER 2

Soccer Basics

Soccer is usually played on a flat, grassy field. The game is also played on beaches and even indoors. At each end of the field is a goal. Each team tries to get the ball into the other team's goal.

When a team gets the ball into the goal, it scores one point. The team that scores the most points wins the game.

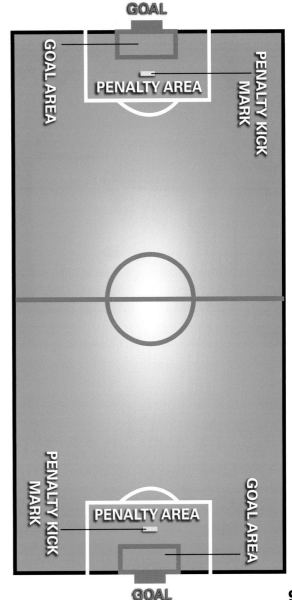

GOAL

GOAL AREA

PENALTY AREA

PENALTY KICK MARK

PENALTY KICK MARK

PENALTY AREA

GOAL AREA

GOAL

A goalie from Martinique flies through the air in a Gold Cup game against El Salvador.

Each team has eleven players on the field. One player is the team's goalkeeper, or goalie. The goalie's job is to stop the ball from going into the goal. The goalie is the only player who can touch the ball with his or her hands.

Other players on the team help the goalie. They are called defenders. Each team has two to four defenders. They usually stay in front of the goal. They try to keep the other team from getting in place to score. When they get the ball, they pass it to the forwards.

Freddy Adu of D.C. United shoots on the New England Revolution's goal.

A Russian player scores a goal against Greece in Portugal.

Forwards spend most of their time at the other end of the field. Their job is to get the ball into the other team's goal. Forwards do most of the scoring. There can be two, three, or four forwards on a team. The best forward is known as the "striker." The striker usually stays toward the center. There, he or she has the best chance of scoring.

The midfielders help the defenders and the forwards. They play both offense and defense, depending on how the game is going. They have to be good at all the jobs on the team. A team can have up to four midfielders.

Who will get there first? Players from both teams rush toward the ball.

Spain and the United States battle for the ball in an Olympic game.

No one player can make a team successful. To win, a team needs more than a great striker or goalie. It needs great teamwork, too. All the players on the team must help each other. They must work well together.

CHAPTER 3

Exciting Plays

Soccer is an action-packed game. Players run
and dodge. They dribble and pass the ball
with their feet.

Players on the other team try to take the ball away. They block shots with their feet, their bodies, and their heads. Soccer players always seem to keep moving.

Brandi Chastain of the United States uses her head in an Olympic gold medal game against Norway.

Goalies often make great saves. They kick the ball. They trap it with their feet. They dive on top of it. They jump up and try to grab it with their hands.

A Manchester United goalie dives to stop a last-minute goal attempt by Newcastle United.

A penalty kick sails over the goalie's arm in a college game.

A penalty kick can give a team a chance to score. A single player has a chance to kick a goal. Only the goalie on the other team can try to stop the ball. A good kicker can make the ball swerve past the goalie and into the goal. Score!

Sometimes a game ends in a tie. The two teams may choose a winner in an exciting way. They may hold a shoot-out. Each team has five chances to score a goal against the other team's goalie. The team that scores the most goals in the shoot-out wins the game.

The pressure is on! A shoot-out can decide which team wins.

CHAPTER 4

World Championships

The most famous soccer trophy is the World Cup. The fight for that trophy takes place every four years. The best women's and men's teams in the world play in the World Cup games.

Olympic soccer is very popular, too. Men's and women's teams from all over the world compete for gold medals.

The U.S. team celebrates its victory over China in the championship game of the FIFA Women's World Cup.

Glossary

amateur – playing a game without being paid for playing

defense – moves made to keep the other team from scoring

offense – moves made in order to score

professionals – people who play a game as a paid job

spectator – to be enjoyed by people who come to watch

For More Information

Books

The History of Soccer. Diana Star Helmer and Thomas S. Owens (Powerkids Press)

K Is for Kick: A Soccer Alphabet. Brad Herzog (Gale Group)

My Soccer Book. Gail Gibbons (HarperCollins)

Soccer Game! Grace Maccarone (Scholastic)

Soccer in Action. Sports in Action (series). Niki Walker and Sarah Dann (Crabtree)

Web Sites

National Soccer Hall of Fame
www.soccerhall.org/games.htm
Online soccer games

Soccer Talk
library.thinkquest.org/5932/INDEX.HTM?tqskip1=1
Information about rules, positions, equipment, and more

Index

About the Author

Jonatha A. Brown has been writing children's books since leaving a corporate position in 2001. She holds a B.A. in English from St. Lawrence University in Canton, New York. Jonny lives in Phoenix, Arizona, where she is a fan of the Arizona Diamondbacks. Her favorite sport is dressage.